# Justin Verlander

By Jeff Savage

AMAZING ATHLETES

Lerner Publications Company • Minneapolis

Lerner Publications Company
A division of Lerner Publishing Group, Inc.
241 First Avenue North
Minneapolis, MN 55401 U.S.A.

Website address: www.lernerbooks.com


Library of Congress Cataloging-in-Publication Data

Justin Verlander / by Jeff Savage.
     p.   cm. — (Amazing athletes)
   Includes index.
   ISBN 978-1-4677-1099-2 (lib. bdg. : alk. paper)
   ISBN 978-1-4677-1108-1 (eBook)
   1. Verlander, Justin—Juvenile literature. 2. Baseball players—United States—Biography—Juvenile literature. I. Title.
GV865.V44S28 2013
796.357092—dc23 [B]                                                    2012033887

Manufactured in the United States of America
1 – BP – 12/31/12

# TABLE OF CONTENTS

Justin Verlander winds up for a pitch on October 16, 2012.

# BEST OF THE BEST

Justin Verlander stood on the **pitcher's mound** in the seventh inning. He looked at his catcher and nodded his head. Justin raised his leg and

fired the baseball toward home plate. Yankees'
batter Robinson Cano swung and missed.
Strike three!

Justin is the **ace** pitcher for the Detroit
Tigers. He and his team were facing the New
York Yankees in the 2012 **American League
Championship Series (ALCS)**. Detroit had the
lead, 2–0. The Tigers had won the first two
games of the series. They had a great chance to
win Game 3 with Justin on the mound.

The crowd watches
Justin on the mound
during the 2012 playoffs.

Justin is one of the best pitchers in **Major League Baseball (MLB)**. He won the Cy Young Award in 2011 as the AL's best pitcher. He was also named Most Valuable Player (MVP) in his league that year. The Yankees knew it wouldn't be easy to beat Justin. "It doesn't get much tougher than Verlander," said New York catcher Russell Martin.

Justin got Raul Ibanez out to end the seventh inning. Then Detroit's ace got three quick outs in the eighth inning. The Tigers still had a 2–0 lead in the ninth inning when Justin took the mound. The first batter was New York's Eduardo Nunez. Justin threw a pitch in the **strike zone**. Bang! Nunez sent the ball over the

Detroit has won the World Series four times: 1935, 1945, 1968, and 1984.

outfield wall for a home run. Detroit's lead was down to 2–1.

Detroit manager Jim Leyland went to the pitcher's mound to talk to Justin. Leyland wanted to make sure Justin wasn't too tired to go on. Justin stayed in the game and got the next out. Then Phil Coke came in for Justin to get the final two outs. Detroit won the game.

Justin talks with manager Jim Leyland *(left)* and catcher Alex Avila *(right)* before leaving the game.

It was a big victory for the Tigers. They were ahead in the series, three games to zero. Detroit would go to the World Series if they could beat the Yankees one more time. But Justin knew that it wasn't yet time to celebrate. "It's great to be up 3–0, but against [the Yankees], you never know," he said. Would the Tigers make it to the World Series?

Justin gives an interview after the game.

Justin grew up in Manakin-Sabot, Virginia. Manakin-Sabot is near Richmond.

# HARD THROWER

Justin Brooks Verlander was born February 20, 1983, in Manakin-Sabot, Virginia. He was raised by his parents, Richard and Kathy. Justin has a younger brother named Benjamin.

Justin was an active boy. He was two when he knocked out his two front teeth. "He tripped on the driveway because he wanted to be first in the car," said Kathy.

Justin earned good grades in school. He liked to raise his hand to give answers. Justin showed little interest in sports as a young boy. He preferred watching television and playing with toys. His dream job was to drive a tractor or dump truck.

Justin had a strong arm. He was six when a neighbor saw him playing catch with a baseball with his father. "Hey, you ought to get that kid in Little League," the neighbor said. A year later, Justin's father threw a rock halfway across a large pond. Justin threw a rock of the same size. It sailed over the pond. Justin's father realized his son had a gift.

A restaurant in Goochland, Virginia, sells a "Verlander Burger." Justin likes the idea more than the hamburger itself. "It has raw onions and tomatoes, and I don't like either one," he said.

Justin was close to his parents as a child. Here he poses with his mother, Kathy *(left)*, and father, Richard *(right)*, in 2012.

Justin was nine when he joined his first youth baseball team. The coach made him a pitcher. But Justin didn't care what position he played. "He was more worried about his snack after the game," said his father.

Justin threw fast pitches. He struck out plenty of batters. But the baseball didn't always go where he aimed. He hit batters with wild pitches. Some parents complained that he was dangerous. Kids were afraid to stand in the **batter's box**.

Coaches helped Justin learn to control his pitches. Before long, he was nearly unhittable. Justin learned more about the game at the Richmond Baseball Academy near his home. By the age of 13, he could throw a baseball 84 miles per hour. He made the varsity team as a freshman at Goochland High School in 1998. His fastball was clocked at 86 miles per hour.

Justin's friends told him he would become a pro baseball player someday. One day at school, Justin was short 50 cents for chocolate milk. He borrowed the money from his friend Daniel

Hicks. Justin promised to repay the money, plus a small part of his future pro baseball **signing bonus**. Daniel wrote the deal on a napkin. Justin laughed and signed it.

Three years later, Justin was hurling fastballs at 90 miles per hour. He struck out 144 batters in 72 innings in 2001. But then he got sick and had to stop playing. When he returned to the baseball field, his fastball had slowed down. Pro **scouts** stopped coming to his games. No team offered him a contract to join the **minor leagues**. Justin went to college instead.

Baseball scouts such as these look for the next great MLB players.

Old Dominion University is in Norfolk, Virginia.

# SETTING RECORDS

Justin started classes at Old Dominion University in Virginia. He was no longer sick. He could throw his blazing fastball again. As a freshman in 2002, he led the Colonial Athletic Association (CAA) with a 1.90 **earned run average (ERA)**. In one game, he struck out 17 batters.

Justin began lifting weights as a sophomore. He reached his full height of 6 feet 5 inches. He weighed 200 pounds. Justin led the CAA with 139 strikeouts. This was a new school record for a season.

Justin was picked to play for Team USA in the 2003 Pan American Games. He pitched against teams from other countries. He recorded a 5–1 record with a 1.29 ERA. He helped the United States win the silver medal.

Justin *(left)* with teammates from Team USA in 2003.

Justin's fastball reached 95 miles per hour in 2004. He had learned several tricky pitches, such as a **curveball** and a **slider**. He struck out 17 batters in one game and 16 in another. He broke his own school record with 151 strikeouts.

Justin was at the top of his game. It was time for a new challenge. He decided to skip his senior year to turn pro. The Detroit Tigers held the second pick of the 2004 MLB **Draft**. They chose Justin.

Justin *(right)* talks with Detroit Tigers president Dave Dombrowski *(left)* in 2004.

The Tigers and Justin's **agent** drew up a **contract**. Justin received a rich deal. It included a signing bonus of more than $3 million. Justin remembered the deal he had signed on a napkin with his friend in high school. Justin wrote a check to Daniel for $3,120.50.

Justin throws a pitch during spring training in February 2005.

Justin started pitching in the minor leagues. He opened the 2005 season with the Class A Lakeland Flying Tigers. In 13 games, he had a record of 9–2 with a 1.67 ERA. He was brought up to the Class AA Erie SeaWolves. He pitched 25 straight innings without allowing a run. The Tigers decided Justin was ready. They called him up to the **major leagues**.

Justin made his big-league start against the Cleveland Indians on July 4, 2005. He gave up four runs and seven hits. After one more game, he told the team **trainer** that his shoulder was sore. The Tigers took no chances. They kept Justin off the field for the rest of the season.

Justin pitches in his second major-league game on July 23, 2005.

Justin showed impressive skills as a rookie in 2006.

# SUPERSTAR

Justin had only pitched in two MLB games in 2005. This meant he was still a **rookie** in 2006. He pitched more like a **veteran**. His fastball reached speeds of over 100 miles per hour. His curveball broke sharply. His slider fooled many batters.

Justin became the first rookie in history to win 10 games before the end of June. Other teams were impressed. "That kid has so much potential, and he doesn't look a bit like a rookie," said Tampa Bay Rays coach Joe Madden.

Justin stays calm during his first playoff game.

Justin finished the season with a record of 17–9. The Tigers were headed to the **playoffs**. Justin beat the New York Yankees in his first playoff game, 4–3. The Tigers won the series to move to the next round. Next up were the Oakland A's.

Justin won Game 2 against Oakland, and Detroit took the series in four games. The Tigers were going to the World Series!

Justin pitched Game 1 of the 2006 World Series against the St. Louis Cardinals. He struck out eight batters in five innings. He also gave up seven runs. The Cardinals won the game. Justin pitched better in Game 5. But he made a costly throwing error, and the Tigers lost again. The Cardinals won the World Series.

Justin throws a pitch during the 2006 World Series.

Justin collects cars. His favorites include a Ferrari, a Maserati, an Aston Martin, and a Mercedes SLS.

Justin and the Tigers were disappointed. But it was a great first year for the young pitcher. Justin was named Rookie of the Year. He was outside washing his car when he heard the news. He came in the house to find 20 missed calls on his phone. Rather than celebrate, he returned to his driveway. "I had to go out and finish washing my car," said Justin. "Can't leave the soap on there."

Justin was great again in 2007. He won 10 times before the **All-Star Game**. One of those wins was the first **no-hitter** at Comerica Park in Detroit. Justin struck out 12 Milwaukee Brewers in the game.

Justin celebrates with teammates after pitching nine innings without giving up a hit.

Justin was chosen for the All-Star Game for the first time in 2007. He finished the season with an 18–6 record. He also led the league in wild pitches and hit batters. "He's a guy no one wants to face," said teammate Brandon Inge. Justin became the first pitcher in history to win Rookie of the Year, pitch in a World Series and an All-Star Game, and throw a no-hitter in his first two seasons. "He's going to be a superstar in this game for a long time," said teammate Ivan Rodriguez.

Justin slipped to an 11–17 record in 2008. The Tigers finished last in the **AL Central Division**. He bounced back in 2009 with a 19–9 record. His 269 strikeouts led the majors. Justin was rewarded with a five-year contract for $80 million. He was given use of a **suite** at Comerica Park for all games. Justin had plans for the suite.

Justin and the Tigers struggled in 2008.

Justin won the Triple Crown of pitching in 2011. He led the league in wins (24), strikeouts (250), and ERA (2.40). He won the AL Cy Young Award as the best pitcher in the league. He became the first pitcher in 19 years to win the MVP award.

Justin has won 124 games since 2006. No other MLB pitcher has won as many games.

Detroit made the playoffs. Justin pitched in two of five games to help the Tigers beat the Yankees in the first round. Then he pitched twice against the Texas Rangers. Justin won Game 5 to keep his team alive. But the Tigers lost the next game to end their season.

Justin came back strong in 2012 with another winning record. He pitched in the All-Star Game. The Tigers reached the playoffs again.

The team rolled through Oakland and New York to reach the World Series. But Detroit had a hard time scoring runs against the San Francisco Giants. The Giants won the World Series in four games.

Justin is one of the best pitchers in the world. But he knows he can get even better. "I'm hoping to learn something new every day," Justin says. "I'm hoping to be in the Hall of Fame."

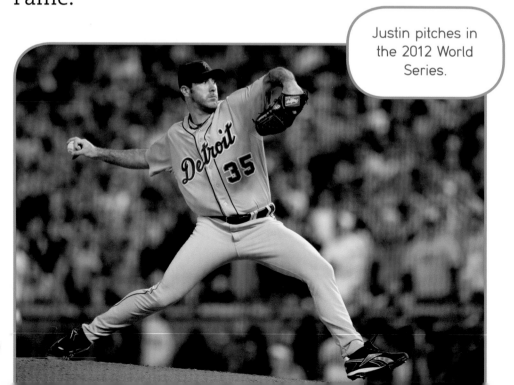

Justin pitches in the 2012 World Series.

# Selected Career Highlights

**2012**   Named to the AL All-Star Game

**2011**   Named AL MVP
Named AL Cy Young Award winner
Led the AL in wins (24), strikeouts (250), and ERA
  (2.40)
Pitched a no-hitter against the Toronto Blue Jays
Named to the AL All-Star Game

**2010**   Named to the AL All-Star Game

**2009**   Led the AL in wins (19) and strikeouts (269)
Finished third in voting for AL Cy Young
  Award
Named to the AL All-Star Game

**2008**   Started 33 games, fifth-most in the AL

**2007**   Pitched a no-hitter against the Milwaukee Brewers
Named to the AL All-Star Game

**2006**   Named AL Rookie of the Year

**2005**   Made his first major-league start on July 4 against the Cleveland
  Indians
Named the Tigers organization minor-league Player of the Year

**2004**   Named First-Team All-CAA
Set a school record and led the CAA with 151 strikeouts
Set a career CAA record with 427 strikeouts

**2003**   Helped Team USA win a silver medal at the Pan American Games
Named First-Team All-CAA
Struck out 17 batters against James Madison University
Struck out 16 batters against Virginia Commonwealth University
Set a school record and led the CAA with 139 strikeouts

**2002**   Named CAA Rookie of the Year
Struck out 17 batters against James Madison University

# Glossary

**ace:** in baseball, the pitcher who is the top starter on a team

**agent:** a person who represents an athlete and handles financial matters

**AL Central Division:** one of the three groups of teams that make up the AL. The AL Central is made up of the Chicago White Sox, the Cleveland Indians, the Detroit Tigers, the Kansas City Royals, and the Minnesota Twins.

**All-Star Game:** a game played in the middle of each season, featuring the top players of the American League and the National League

**American League Championship Series (ALCS):** a set of games played at the end of the baseball season between the top two teams in the American League. The team that wins four games goes to the World Series.

**batter's box:** the rectangular area on either side of home plate in which the batter stands while at bat

**contract:** a deal agreed to and signed by a player and a team that includes the amount of money the player will earn and the number of years the player will play

**curveball:** a slower pitch that dives downward as it approaches home plate

**draft:** a yearly event in which high school and college players are chosen by teams

**earned run average (ERA):** the number of runs a pitcher allows per nine innings. For example, if a pitcher pitches nine innings and gives up three runs, the pitcher's ERA would be 3.00.

**Major League Baseball (MLB):** the top group of professional men's baseball teams in North America, divided into the National League and the American League

**major leagues:** the top level of professional baseball

**minor leagues:** a series of teams in which players gain experience and improve their skills before going to the major leagues

**no-hitter:** a game in which the pitcher does not allow any batter to reach base safely on a hit

**pitcher's mound:** a dirt hill in the shape of a circle about 60 feet from home plate on which the pitcher stands

**playoffs:** a series of games after the regular season to determine a champion

**rookie:** a first-year player

**scouts:** experts whose job is to watch players in high school and college to determine if they are worthy of being offered a contract to join a professional sports team

**signing bonus:** extra money paid to a player, in addition to a yearly salary, for signing a contract to join a professional sports team

**slider:** a pitch that drops downward and sideways as it approaches home plate

**strike zone:** the square area above home plate, generally between both sides and between the batter's knees and chest

**suite:** rooms at sports stadiums that are set aside for use by certain people during games

**trainer:** a person in charge of maintaining the physical health of players

**veteran:** a player with more than one year of experience

## Further Reading & Websites

Fishman, Jon M. *Miguel Cabrera*. Minneapolis: Lerner Publications Company, 2013.

Kennedy, Mike, and Mark Stewart. *Long Ball: The Legend and Lore of the Home Run*. Minneapolis: Millbrook Press, 2006.

Savage, Jeff. *Prince Fielder*. Minneapolis: Lerner Publications Company, 2013.


The Official Site of the Detroit Tigers
http://detroit.tigers.mlb.com/index.jsp?c_id=det
The Detroit Tigers official site includes the team schedule and game results, late-breaking news, biographies of Justin Verlander and other players and coaches, and much more.

The Official Site of Major League Baseball
http://www.mlb.com
Major League Baseball's official website provides fans with the latest scores and game schedules, as well as information on players, teams, and baseball history.

*Sports Illustrated Kids*
http://www.sikids.com
The *Sports Illustrated Kids* website covers all sports, including baseball.

# Index

# Photo Acknowledgments

The images in this book are used with the permission of: © Mark Cunningham/MLB Photos/Getty Images, pp. 4, 8, 20, 25, 29; © Gregory Shamu/Getty Images, p. 5; AP Photo/Matt Slocum, p. 7; © Bill Cobb/SuperStock, p. 9; © Jonathan Daniel/Getty Images, p. 11; © Matt May/US Presswire, p. 13; © iStockphoto.com/Tiffany Morrison, p. 14; Peter Jones/Reuters/Newscom, p. 15; AP Photo/Paul Sancya, p. 16; Charles W Luzier/Reuters/Newscom, p. 17; AP Photo/Duane Burleson, p. 18; © Michael Zagaris/MLB Photos/Getty Images, p. 19; © Robert Caplin/Bloomberg/Getty Images, p. 21; AP Photo/Duane Burleson, p. 23; © Michael Sachett/US Presswire, p. 24; ZUMA Press/Newscom, p. 26; © Brad Mangin/MLB Photos/Getty Images, p. 28.

Front cover: © Leon Halip/Getty Images.

Main body text set in Caecilia LT Std 55 Roman 16/28.
Typeface provided by Adobe Systems.